Already Dead
Live Now

Already Dead Live Now

AUSTIN DUMAS

All rights reserved. No part of this publication may be reproduced, distributed, or transmitted in any form by any means, including photocopying, recording, or other electronic methods without the prior written permission of the author, except in the case of brief quotations embodied in reviews and certain other noncommercial uses permitted by copyright law. For permission requests, write to the author at the address below.

Copyright © 2023 Austin Lamar Dumas
austin.l.dumas@gmail.com

ISBN 979-8-218-09653-3

Edited and designed by Tell Tell Poetry

Printed in the United States of America

First Printing, 2023

I dedicate this book of poems to family, friends, and folks on planet earth full of hope or in need of hope.

"Know thyself."

—inscribed in the Temple of Apollo at Delphi

CONTENTS

I. MIRROR

Evolution Song	5
Bridge	6
Breaking Down	7
Breaking The Natural Law	8
Thus Spoke Human Miracles	9
Naivety	10
Mother's Comet	11
Construct	12
Consensus Reality	13
Sacred Rage	14
Opium	16
The Kid's Manifesto	17
Memento Mori	18
Amor Fati	20
A Film	21
Atlas	22
I Exist	23
Innocence Lost	24
Rotten Teeth	25
Black Magic	26
Imperfection Is Perfect	27
Parable Of The Insane Children	28
Mystical May Be Logic	29
Honoring The Mysteries Of The Universe	30
You Are You	31
Surrender	32
Reborn	33
It Doesn't Matter	34
My Friend	35

II. ENTANGLE

Dreaming Of You	39

Love Stories	40
Oasis	42
My Beloved Angel	43
Venus Rising	44
Freya	46
Michelle	47
I Adore You And Me	48
Interconnected	49
Somebody To Love	50
Fate Weaves A Spiderweb	51
Snowfall	52
Fool For You	53
Time Paradox	54
Playing Against Time	55
Rock Bottom	56
The Absurd Hero	57
Being Human Is A Guest House	58
Viva La Vida	59
Everyday Life	60
Everything Is Divine	62
All People Shared The World, Part 1	63
All People Shared The World, Part 2	64
Alive	65
Songs And Myths Of Myself, Part 1	67
Songs And Myths Of Myself, Part 2	68
Birthday	69
Unconditional Love	70
Freedom	71

III. TRANSFORM

Remember Yourself	75
God Bless The Breath Of Life	76
Naming It	78
Transformation	80
Breathing Is Law	81
Arriving	82
Spirit Songs	83

Invisible Self	84
Divine Departure	85
Wherever You Go, There You Are	86
Lotus Blossom	87
Stream Of Consciousness	88
Sake Poetry, Part 1	89
Sake Poetry, Part 2	90
Sake Poetry, Part 3	91
Inherited Will	93
The Great Beyond	94
Yoga	95
Already Dead Live Now	96
The End	98

Already Dead
Live Now

1.
MIRROR

EVOLUTION SONG

I know living isn't easy.
The sun will scorch your flesh.
The rain will drown your flowers.
People will tell you lies.
Loved ones will scar your heart.

I know living isn't easy.
Our pain feels like
it will last forever.
We're seeds raised by agony.
One day we'll become a tree
that feels it is impossible
to be free.

I know living isn't easy.
Bodies will bathe in a flaming baptism
and burn to a crisp turning the skies gray,
purifying air with the smell of hellfire and sulfur.
But in the next daylight you will return
and grow again,
reaching towards the sun's open arms as a seed song.

I know living isn't easy.
The axman will cut you in two.
Dying seems easier.
But it's not the end.
Keep growing and keep going.
Even when you feel like you can't.
You're a beautiful seed song
of creation:
a great work in progress
still singing.

BRIDGE

What divides you from the other?
Clothes?
Skin color?
Wealth or health?
Weight or height?
Age or beliefs?
Social class or sexuality?
Is it a story in your mind,
that separates you from the other?
Imagine this, inside of you:
you have a heart pumping blood
throughout your body,
keeping you alive.
If you pierce through your skin
and tear a hole in your heart,
all your blood will leak out.
We are the same inside.
We are fragile and doomed
with the same fate.
That fact alone should bring us together.
Build a bridge, one to the other.

BREAKING DOWN

Are you the one
to break me down?
To break down my identity,
my habits,
my behavior?
To break down my justifications for living—
the reason my brain resists
and tics like mechanical clock?

Are you the one
to make me feel real,
alive and alleviated?
Are you the reason
for this experience within
the corrosion of my skin,
as if my fallibility is forever
dissolved?
As if my mortality
isn't eating me
from the inside out?
You're tearing out the petals
of your flowers,
and once you're uprooted
from the earth,
we cannot be replanted or
replaced.

Are you the one?
The one to fracture me into
my most basic elements?
To distill my inner desires
into a satiable substance
and reform me
into something new?
Something beyond mundane.
Something true.

BREAKING THE NATURAL LAW

Silly human animals
breaking the natural law of nature
and the universe.

Silly culture creatures creating
totalitarian myths and moralities
to control and conquer nature and the universe,

silly parasites thinking you're so big
as you plunge into the ground
and deprive resources from other creatures.

Silly tyrants planting make-believe signs
into the land,
claiming it's your private property
and in your possession.

None of your subjective world theories
are true to nature.
They're just fabricated principles
constructed to control nature.
And while you're endeavoring to destroy nature,
you're hurting yourself.

THUS SPOKE HUMAN MIRACLES

Praise the human miracles!
The human miracles are the only animals
to go insane by their own sentience.

The human miracles are the only animals
that speak about their isolation
and starvation for spiritual communion.

The human miracles are the only animals
to play symbolic games of morality
and force other animals to participate.

I'm seeing the greatest minds of my time
sell their souls to controlled hallucinations.
The human miracles dive into water
to gather glowing objects of desire
or demise.

NAIVETY

In first grade, I wrote a letter
to the president of the United States,
the current leader of the free world.

Who are we as a nation?
And why aren't we working towards
a collective unity under one sky?
Why are we destroying trees
and replacing them with structures
that don't contribute to our ability to breathe?

Why are we building cathedrals of capital power?
Are we fighting for freedom?
Why are we replacing natural organisms
with phallic skyscrapers?

I'm a first grader, so maybe I'm ignorant.
Mr. President, since you're an adult, maybe you can you tell me
what humanity's number one priority is?

Is it collective consumption without end, or
is it cultivating human existence?

Does the human animal subconsciously have malice for itself?
It seems to pursue its personal self-destruction
derived from a deep-seated search for a piece of the soul
and a desire to dominate its insecurities.

I grew up to realize we're deviant, and miraculous spectacles, and spectators
of our demise, and divinity,
destiny, and deeds.
We can choose clarity.

MOTHER'S COMET

Have you heard the news?
Armageddon is coming soon.
The old games we play—
ravaging Mother Earth will end.
It's written in the stars, embellished in obsidian skies.
Our great mother is purging it all to rubble.

Pagan priests pray
for a comet to fall like rain—
but hope the comet
brings collective unity
before our united demise.

No more rational mind tricks
or manipulation of the market.
No more greedy nobles
taking without giving
like mosquitos in the summer heat.
No more hungry orphans
going through an anorexic metamorphosis.

No more West versus East.
No more blue team versus red team.
No dichotomies or ideologies.
In our final hour, will it be too late
to ask ourselves, *do we deserve this?*

CONSTRUCT

Have you ever pondered the curious things humans do?
One of the weirdest things we humans do
that other animals don't do
is make up social constructs.
Our names.
Money.
Poverty.
Politics.
Nations.
Religions.
Capitalism.
Corporations.
Racism.
Maybe America should have a better educational system
and have a class on racism.
Maybe then it wouldn't be a practice anymore?

CONSENSUS REALITY

Reality is a
social contract
between humans.
If you break it,

you're not tearing off
wings of an archangel
of a divine order.

You're breaking
the vows
of human order.

Chaos seeps through,
like a mirage.
And we agree on
what we want to name it.

SACRED RAGE

He can't breathe,
        can you hear him?

He said he can't breathe!
            There's murder in the streets

caused by those meant to protect
            and serve.

Morality bleeds out
        all over American soil.

Generations come to soak it up
            like a wet sponge.

A primal predator, a tiger,
            a government, and parasites play

with our intestines.
        So, let's vote for it to continue

to tear us into pieces
            from the inside out.

Let's pay our blood taxes
              so individuals behind a badge

can pledge allegiance to suspending
              their ethics and logic

in order to impose the wills
              of sociopaths in tailor-made suits.

Policemen sing wicked lullabies.
    A loud and mighty war cry

heard across the world
    comes from minds and bodies in agony.

The collective humanity knows
    the truest color is love—

the language of the soul.
    But old traumas stretched across time

are etched in skins of brothers and sisters
    and carried into the present

by heartless words
    of ignorant terrorists.

Resist repression,
  come into power.

Our sacred rage
    will sing louder. . . .

Ignorance will be a low whisper in cities
    filled with anarchy medicine

as old worlds that perpetuate
    vicious cycles of police brutality

crumble.

OPIUM

We cave-dwelling monkeys,
we united and entitled farmers
sell opium to the masses.

We human consumers
are causes of our own suffering;
we prey on distracting ourselves
like vultures seeking
delicious carcasses.
We want things
that make us feel alive
and full
and special.

To make us feel relieved
and blissful
in ignoring
our impermanence,
as if it's forever.

Give us numb visions
instead of remembering
our grand race against mortality.

THE KID'S MANIFESTO

I always wanted to be a normal kid,
a kid that pretended to be
everything he imaged himself to be:
astronaut,
wrestler,
cowboy,
super hero,
immortal poet;
and vast galaxies
beyond the heavens.

I grew up to be a hot-headed teenager
that wanted to burn the world into ashes.
I was a kid writing a manifesto
on the human condition,
about how we believe we're angels
that want to breed like animals.
But our perfect halos are atomic bombs
ready to blow up and shimmer in the sky.

MEMENTO MORI

His body
drops
dead.
Bodies
drop
dead
all the time.
People talk
to the dead.

His heart
stops
dead.
Our hearts
will stop
dead.
Someday
we'll be
with the dead.

Remember
someday
we will
die.
But now
we're alive.
There's still time
to be alive.

Remember
your death.
When she comes
for you

it will be swift
and quick
like a flash
of lighting,
over in a blink
of an eye,
gone.

Return to
your breath.
When she comes
for you
it may be
a memory
or a dream.
We fade into
rays of light,
gone.

AMOR FATI

Pain is a chain and a navel string
developed at birth,
bound over our throats.
Vexed mystery muffles us.
Life's honey coheres to life's adversity.
We question: gift or curse?

But we can influence
the tides of time
and our fragile fate
by enduring and embracing it.
As seeds for creation—
that is the cure to pain.
Nothing should be changed in our past.
Our future is beyond our control.
This moment is all we have.
Death, our biggest sorrow, solidifies our fate.

A FILM

Beautiful and wicked characters
play games on the cinema screen
while sleepwalking in a daydream.

Beautiful and wicked characters
behave in roles and dramas
like they're bewildered by the way
they're playing out their traumas.

Beautiful and wicked characters
ask, *Why is this happening to me?*
I have a story in my head
telling me to survive at all costs,
as if I already lost,
telling me it's you versus me.
Who wrote this allegory?

Beautiful and wicked characters
breathe in the cosmos
realizing the river of creation
is within our consciousness
and in our ability to attune
and move with nature.
It's not easy burning in the shadows
of our own making—
to realize we're one breath,
experiencing ourselves completely.

ATLAS

When you're first born, no one tells you
fathers can be angry monsters
perpetuating a vicious cycle.
Some children don't know what to do
with pain they're poisoned with
and don't know where to hide it.
So they become angry monsters
and give it to their children
like a disease holding them hostage.

My father made it hard.
Abandoned us, little sisters, brother,
left us alone to defend ourselves,
protect our own selves from life's night terrors.
He left us with just
a small ounce of love, hoped our mother
would take care of us,
and we would live happily ever after.
And like Atlas
I weighted the world on my shoulders.

I EXIST

Sad people tell a little spell about suffering,
being lost in the world
and seeking perfection.

I'd be satisfied just to exist.
Someday I won't.

We come and go like a blue sky.
In the hospital room a newborn is crying.
In a pitch-black room an old man is dying.

Oh world how long do I need to bleed
Oh world you are a swift gift—
before I blink the curtains come down

We're torn vessels—
on the other side
of pain/ misery/ chaos,
there's love/ harmony/ peace.
In the shadows I journey out,
learning to keep alive this *I*,
this *me* that exists in the world.
Without it, nothing would matter.

INNOCENCE LOST

The hardest realization of life
is being born in a world
that gives you a dry and bitter taste
of ignorance and wickedness
as soon as you fall
out of your mother's womb.

Our birthright is mortality,
enfolding its various fickle fingers
around your fragile throat.

You're expected to go along with it,
blindly as if you asked for it
and gave it consent.

Is innocence lost after you
fall out of her womb?

ROTTEN TEETH

Her rotten teeth had bitter bites and contaminated the wounds.
She told vicious verbal lies.
Vexed by vanity, the ego, leaped in our way,
becoming walls without the will to break or climb over.

BLACK MAGIC

She's a pretty pistol aimed at my skull—
my fingers are tempted to pull the trigger.

Her hot metal in my hands feels like a baby fetus
unconsciously numb in mother's womb.

Once we took our first breath
there was a sacred death
in between her thighs.

My veins were cold.
My limbs were severed.
She dipped her hands in my blood.

Death greets me at the door
and she weeps tears of joy.
I have embraced these moments as ecstasy.
Any day could have been my last.
I have lived a full life,
gathering vitality out of the world
that passed me by.

IMPERFECTION IS PERFECT

They were all sentenced
death as a birthright.
Man, with gorilla hands,
sentience of an elephant,
was never meant
to outlive its true nature.
Imperfection is perfect.

The piper plays
to speak to the blood
of the world.
His music enters
through bone, flesh
to know the mortal pain
of living and dying.

Piper plays for truth,
pulse of universe.
Everything is
mutable, like
disintegrating seasons.

Death as birthright.
Man
was never
meant to out-
live
nature.
Imperfection
is perfect.

PARABLE OF THE INSANE CHILDREN

The tragedy was lying there
dead in her arms.
The realization of death
became clear.

The sages have said,
*We're dead when we begin
the journey of life.*

*The lesson we must learn is
to never take life so seriously.
Live as if you lost everything.
Eventually you will have nothing.*

*Stop looking for the fountain of youth.
We are bones and we are dust.
And we are miracles unfolding.*

MYSTICAL MAY BE LOGIC

Our universe
in union with itself
is love—
immensely bigger than
we first conceived.

Maybe no prison concepts
can shackle it
to one theory.
By way of words,
by swoon of sweet nectar
bursting in sentence
and experience,

maybe our *reality*
is just one daydream.

Maybe there's no absolute truth
and we must live with that fact.

HONORING THE MYSTERIES OF THE UNIVERSE

Every day it gets a little harder
to bear witness
to the mistakes we make.

Every day it gets a little better witnessing
the mysteries
of the universe.

The everyday gets blurred together,
and it's difficult feeling the pressure
to spin like a wheel
in a monotonous machine.

But on the days I reflect
and catch up with my breath,
and stop trying to imprison
the divine spark
into a glass jar, like a firefly,

there's not one answer
to reveal all the mysteries of the universe.
I am a small vessel floating
in a vast sea
and what cascades over the horizon
is the infinite unknown.
It's impossible to know everything.

YOU ARE YOU

A unique composition of primordial elements
originating from the core
of decaying stardust beings,
made from the same dynamic
source of energy.

SURRENDER

Surrender to the moment.
It's not easy.
It's easier to twist and shout
to escape the moment.

The past seems more comfortable,
or maybe uncomfortable
depending on your point of view.

To travel into the future
and into a distant dream
seems better than what's happening now.

But here and now is who you are.
And it's not easy
because it's a practice.

REBORN

We are like phoenixes that burn into ashes
and are reborn in the morning,
then at night we die again.

We go through a cycle of life and death
and rebirth in the moment.
Tomorrow you will not be the same person
as yesterday.

You will be a person that has learned new lessons
and lived in another timeline.
Don't fight yourself
for making a mistake in yesterday's life.
Be kind and compassionate,
and forgive yourself.
Fly out of the ashes.
Begin again.

IT DOESN'T MATTER

It doesn't matter—
you can measure
every grain of sand
next to the ocean bed.
Would you really want
to count every particle
in the universe?

If you want to compare or contrast
every piece of information,
issue, and every complex structure,
you should.
But it may take
the rest of your life
to do so.

All things that exist are temporary,
yet it's worth the ride
that goes up and down,
sideways and backwards.
And you vomit a little,
but it's just a ride
that you'll eventually
get off of.

Don't take it seriously
all the time.
It doesn't matter.
This perfect illusion shall pass.

MY FRIEND

My friend, I read your book that day;
one hand held the spine
and the other embraced your face softly.
As I kissed your lips
our apocalypse uncovered
true intimacy and brilliant beauty.

Our blood boiled over the horizon.
Our hearts knocked on our skin walls
and demanded to be set free.
The space in between became small.

Our breath became one.
One earth, air, fire, water, and spirit.
All the elements I unearthed
to read the contents of your story.

I read and read and released
the space in between us.
And I'll continue to read the trilogy
until I read the words: *the end*.

11.
ENTANGLE

DREAMING OF YOU

I've seen her before,
    somewhere familiar.
It's on the tip of my tongue.
    On edges of my skin.
I know that ancient feeling—
    the touch of her voice.
Riding through my veins
    and in my blood.
Exploring the inner mines
    of my mind.
She's a subconscious kiss;
    her bright pink hair and her disco glamour
brings a familiar warmth.
    Maybe it's somewhere inside,
a phantasmagoric house
    of infinite mirrors.

In the theater room,
    everything seems familiar,
filled with everyone I met and knew.
    They're all visitors looking for somewhere
to sit.

On the cinema screen,
    she's singing the crowd's favorite song
from the movie of our lives.
She sounds pristine and illuminating
    like an evanescent night
showing me hope of sunlight.
    A dream-vision, an echo
coursing inside my head.

LOVE STORIES

I love you.
I have loved you ever since
my sun aligned with your moon.
Ever since you were the first star
shimmering in the night sky.

I imagined we first met
when all the atoms in the universe
reached the highest crescendo,
crashing together into one point,
then expanding into what is now creation.

I imagined it was there
that my atoms and your atoms
embraced and encircled each other
as one substance
conceiving the universe.

Are you swimming here too?
And lost in the immensity
of our ocean eyes?
Are we magnetized
by the rise and fall
of our minds and souls
being mesmerized?

Life is too short to ignore
the intimate pulses
of our hearts caught in a trance,
caught in this sacred dance of electricity,
in our fingertips
and in the touch
of your lips.

This familiar kiss.
This profound abyss.

My atoms and your atoms exist
connected by this
invisible bond.
My atoms feel like
they've known your atoms since forever.

OASIS

That lovely night,
urges creeped in, like
a legion of locusts,
swarming with wild passion,
with moist lips and
tongues tied.

Red wine saturated
our amorous thirst
and organized an oasis.
To let loose in
for our waning skins.

MY BELOVED ANGEL

My beloved, we are like
the true mamas and papas of the world,
tending to our garden
of miracles and dramas
with patience,
communicating compassion and empathy.
And mending broken parts of our home,
building the foundation together.

My beloved, we have long talks in the night
before the morning light breaks through our windows.
Through the beautiful and ugly reflections
we move along.

My beloved, I'm not afraid, for I'm not alone.
You're there at the end of time by my bedside,
holding my hand and nurturing my spirit
before I sleep away the world.
Taking care of me as I age to dust.
And I'm present in your elder years
as you rest your head
on my heart and chest
to sleep away the world.

My beloved, you know who I am.
You knew when we first kissed.
Angels leaped off your tongue
and touched mine;
you knew then my solitude
wouldn't be my own.
And my love would be vast.

VENUS RISING

What is beauty?
Could she be
an adrenaline-rush
in your fingertips?
Could she be
lust looming on your lips,
seducing you into a state of instant pleasure
insinuated by the sway of her tongue?
Could she be
desire conveyed in the pendulum
swing of her hips?

What is beauty?
Could she be
that delicious bite of a
decadent chocolate, drenched
in caramel, and complimented
by a hot cup of coffee?

What is beauty?
Could she be
the rise and fall of the sun beaming?
An explosion of colors: blue, pink, orange
and violet?

Could she be
discovered in a wide-eyed child that's elevated
by pure wonderment at the sight
of a rainbow,
as if it were seen for the first time?

What is beauty?
Could she be
decoded in the brilliant symphonies
of birds, violins, pianos, Bach, Beethoven, or the Beatles,
as if music were heard for the first time?
What is beautiful to you?

FREYA

It's been years since I've felt
your touch, your evocative warmth.
Our bodies embraced, never lost
the rhythm of existing as one,
like cells miraculously merging.

Angels sing in accordance with the heavens,
but you've been the only one—
the only one that made me feel
something unfathomable
like liquid slipping through
ethereal hands.

Your eyes mirror galaxies and nebulas.
Our kiss was in space; we alone experienced.
I died every time I loved you,
to be reborn every day.
I was smoldered inside your
combusting sun.

Your soft lips were a void
and a salvation.
All I ever want is for you to be happy.
If that's with another, I have no choice
but to compromise
because you gave me a world.
You showed me love wasn't a secret.

MICHELLE

Michelle,
your vigorous voice hit a warm crescendo
and stitched onto my blistering, bone-chilling body
on this withering winter night.
And now my brain starts to rattle with riddles
that seem to have no ending.

I got lost swimming in the cobalt blue,
starlight spirals of your eyes.
I fell deeply into your mammoth orbit
and was dragged by your magnetic gravity.
I drowned in the cocktails that you cooked
and was serenaded by the release of serotonin
and endorphins coming out of every pore.

Michelle,
you're a sly and shrewd fox
that slipped pass the cracks and crevices
of my ruined walls
and left footprints around the forest of my mind
throughout this cold and white winter.
Now I wait for your return.

I ADORE YOU AND ME

We can get lost in ourselves
and play a beautiful game
in a world of enchantment
where we hide and seek
our other piece of the puzzle.

We play the price
to tremble and be enamored
by the touch of skin,
by who we are within.
And by embracing your truth
inside the mirror.

INTERCONNECTED

We're interconnected
by an invisible string,
an amorphous force
that's interwoven
in the codes
and designs of our skins.

We're entangled
and enchanted
by the web of fate
that's written in our eyes.
We're animating
the universe,
defined in our eyes.

SOMEBODY TO LOVE

We were listening to Jefferson Airplane,
"Somebody to Love."
I told her I loved her with my body
but not my heart.
I wanted to somebody to love,
but I was a liar
shrouded in loneliness.

Now I wear that mistake
like a layer of skin.

FATE WEAVES A SPIDERWEB

Fate weaves a spiderweb

and we are butterflies

caught in the center.

We have high hopes

that by moving our wings

reality will change

in our favor.

SNOWFALL

Under a glaring moonlight
snow fell with the weight
to freeze hell over.

Two distant lovers
were frostbitten and forbidden
to meet again,
sanctioned by the old laws
of their villages.

Two distant lovers
didn't listen to rules—
instead, they were lead
by their heartbeats
and by a rush of blood.

The cold was felt in their bones.
But even fate couldn't restrict
love unbounded.
Every moment they had
could be their last chance
to embrace and keep warm.

This intimacy burns
within their bodies.
The snowfall and old laws
didn't crush their passion.
It was the distance
that made them shudder in sorrow.
Death encountered them both
entangled and frozen,
under a glaring moonlight.

FOOL FOR YOU

I'm a fool for you.
Always been a fool for you,
but we're not together, not anymore.
I drift around like a ghost for you.

These days I'm not believing
in the seasons anymore.
These days I'm not believing
in something new.
I'm not believing in changes anymore.
No more messiahs or pursuits of happiness.
These days I'm not believing in morning light
or bird songs to wake me from the night.

I tell myself, *Forget about this life.*
It's a death sentence anyways.
I'm lost in this vast maze
hoping to feel alive
and hoping to find my way back to you,
believing in nothing but your touch.

TIME PARADOX

Time skeptics
gleam into the past
to cradle nostalgia

hoping to restart
and go back.
To freeze history.

I can't bind time, love,
and live forever.
This is it.

Our avatars crumble and collapse,
moving through space and time.
But what if I told you

these bodies make it difficult
to perceive time
as a simple mirage,
crystalized in eternity?

Death invested in our mortal shells
the first day we opened our spry eyes.
But it's possible
our spirits can be lifted
in gusts of butterfly wings
causing worlds to collide and rise.

In the presence of hummingbirds
fluttering and slowing down,
this hour and this minute,
second by second,
we're getting older and changing.
We cherish this moment
as if it were our last.

PLAYING AGAINST TIME

I've had a bone to pick with you
since my birth.
Even before I was a festering thought
floating in my parents' minds,
I've been blessed with sentience
to consciously perceive my mortal departure—
my slow descent into dust powder
whisking in the wind.

You are
an itch I can't scratch.
You are
a relentless, agonizing antagonist.
You are
my opponent in this chess game of life.
You are
fundamentally two steps ahead of me.

Over the years, I've learned
a secret to this chess game
and found a way to checkmate your king:
Accept my fate.
Let go and dive into the eternal now.
Tomorrow isn't absolute.
Allow the mutable laws of nature
to take its course.

ROCK BOTTOM

Look deep down into the eyes of the canyon,
like an intimate lover.
Don't turn away from your fear.
It's possible you'll solve
the riddle of who am I
within the chaos.

What trauma makes your skin crawl?
Where are your wounds
that bleed out your essence?
Who hurt you?
Facing these questions
seems like hitting rock bottom.

But maybe they're opportunities
to move through the thick layers
of soil and through the layers of rock,
to connect with the core of
the earth and who you truly are.

Are you holding your past lived trauma close?
Like a talisman,
hoping it protects you?
Are your heart wounds bleeding
all over the place
when you talk to others?

Are you keeping them close,
the ones that hurt you?
What happens if you let go
of the pain you hold tight?

Make the unconscious, conscious.
Illuminate the shadows at the bottom
of the canyon.
What do you see?

THE ABSURD HERO

What if our human condition is to live in a barren wasteland
without an ultimate meaning to our existence
and to our withering mortal coils?

Some of us rise at dawn,
skip breakfast, get in our cars,
spend four or eight hours or more
worshipping our job,
maybe some lunch, and some more worshipping,
back into the car, dinner, then sleep to repeat:
the mundane cycles and rhythm of
Mondays, Tuesdays, Wednesdays, Thursdays,
Fridays, Saturdays, and Sundays.

The absurd festers in our veins
reflecting our innate futility.
We collapse under the pressure
and the hold of this meaningless abyss.
What's the point of life if this is all it is?

These questions put you face to face
with the realization that there is no absolute answer;
these questions put you face to face at a crossroad.
Thoughts churn and churn and churn, like a moving train.
Do I give up? Do I throw it all away?
A choice must be made while we're trapped
in our stark straitjacket, drowning in this pool of chaos.

Here's an alternative: keep the absurd alive and breathing.
Contemplate the absurd in your consciousness.
Accept and embrace the absurd by reaching into the abyss
and taking out and carving your own personal meaning of life.
Mine is to laugh at the absurd often.
That's one meaning of life.
Choose your own.

BEING HUMAN IS A GUEST HOUSE

Rumi writes, *being human
is a guest house.*
Let's be entertained by
our momentary awareness
and our visitors.

I'm so happy you're here.
It feels less lonely.
But everything is temporary
and everything comes with a price.

I'm so happy!
Happy you came to my guest house
to clear me out,
rob me of my joy
in the cold of night.
And at dawn bathe me in your drizzle delight.
I'm so grateful for this guide
that comes and goes.

I welcome your arrival:
malice and shame,
peace and love,
the condemnation, the gluttony, and the envy;
the taste of ecstasy and pleasure
from the touch of a lover;
thunderstorms of the mind
and the gentle sense of stillness
passing through you as you watch
your precious child sleep in serenity.
I welcome it all!

VIVA LA VIDA

Is life a complex puzzle?
Is life a perpetual mystery
that keeps expanding
the moment you're in on it?

Long live life again and again!
Live, and enjoy the days
full of sublime sentiments
and vigorous virtues!
Revel in the days
full of scornful smog
casting a long shadow.

It doesn't matter if you think it's a puzzle,
or a mystery, or a question to be answered.
It's possible you'll see the answer
and gain nothing at the end of your life.

Perhaps it's not a complex puzzle
that can be solved one time
and then finished.
Perhaps it's an absurd cycle of
waking up every day
and solving it again.

EVERYDAY LIFE

Every day
people spend their free time

wondering
how to spend it,

wandering
toward dead ends,

wasting all their time
in search
of freeing their minds.

Searching
for the meaning
of their one life to live.

I see how they get lost
in the midst
of lovers and friends,

telling stories
of how they climb
the tallest mountains of pain.

And the risks they took.
And the mistakes they made

and the loss
and the cost
of living on.

Before it's over,
you bet there were a few doubts
about how it will turn out.

And whether it was all worth it,
worth the struggle to keep on going,

before flowers fade
and bones settle in the dirt.

EVERYTHING IS DIVINE

If you listen ever so closely
to the person next to you,
their soul could come alive
through the texture of their voice,
through the contents of their mind.

The everyday man and woman;
friends, family, neighbors, enemies.
Corporate capitalist hoarders,
middle-class workers
working towards their graves
or until their backs are broken
are divine!
Even the poor, lonely, and homeless,
rolling dice,
hoping luck is on their side
are divine!

At the end of the day
and at the end of our lives,
we're howling at the world.
Howling to be shown the light,
crying and hoping our choices
and deeds are meaningful and divine.
We're all together crying,
Everything is divine!

ALL PEOPLE SHARED THE WORLD PART 1

Exhausted, yearning, roaming
in this wasteland,
wishing for connection,
limitless freedom, undying
love, immortalization—to feel
completely understood.

Have we been tricked?
Will we ever grasp
what truth means?

I lay my head on her chest,
harmonize with her being.
She just wants me to listen
to her heart, to her stories.
Her heart, her stories sound a cascade,
like a strong and tranquil waterfall.

I say, *You are not alone,*
your existence means the world to me.
It makes me happy you're alive.

ALL PEOPLE SHARED THE WORLD PART 2

The whole wide world,
everyone in every country,
the sacred, the politicians,
the peacekeepers, the lawmen,
the anarchists, the soldiers,
the enemies, the lovers,
the abusers, the jokesters,
the rich, and poor,
the old, and young,
the children and the dying
are all working on
being okay with the agonizing
loneliness of living
with that existential question of
what is the point of this?
What if the purpose is to not call it work?
And realize it's to just play and have fun.

Play with me for a moment and imagine
no made-up borders,
no boundaries separating you
from the other.
Imagine *the other* doesn't exist:
it's just you in a relationship with you.
Imagine all the people
sharing the world,
and *have a blessed day*
wasn't just something
to say after departing.
It would be as if people
shared the world together.

ALIVE

What a life
fading and wasting away,
fast and slow into
who knows?

Sweeping and sweeping
the kitchen floor again.
Working and working
until it's time to clock out and go home.

Bills and bills
better pay or else
you won't survive this cold world.

Swimming and swimming
in a monotonous pool
of the living dead.

Taste seems ordinary
and stale, like ash.
The view seems ordinary.
The smell of burning winter wood
and the heat it brings
seems ordinary too.

It gets old,
tossing and turning in bed,
trying to sleep
before the alarm goes off
and screams at you
to get back on the hamster wheel.

It gets tiresome trying to beat the clock
and remove its hands
from strangling you to death.
Is this life, this reality, a long con?
What does it mean to be alive?

A gentle touch of your fingers
caressing my chest
sends shock waves
full of staggering sensations
through my body.
My heart dances with that magic
like there's no tomorrow,
like a child jumping for joy at recess.

I am alive, I am alive!
Drinking your sweet juice
from your naked fruits.
I am alive, I am alive!
Breathing you in, like oxygen.

SONGS AND MYTHS OF MYSELF PART 1

I am here now!
Here to be enraptured and ravaged.
Here to be myself
especially since everyone else is already taken
and celebrating their own sense of glory.

I am here now!
Here to be a particle of God.
Here to be a miracle of the universe,
birthed to be earthly elements
and elements of stars.
Here to be one with every atom
that holds this human structure together.

Here to be every atom
that belongs to me.
The atoms that belong to me
have a reason to be.
If I wasn't meant to exist,
then I wouldn't have
the awareness or experience
that I am here, now.

SONGS AND MYTHS OF MYSELF PART 2

We live here and now
inside a paradox's womb.

We are legends
converging with the changing self.

We allow the emergence of heaven.
Meanwhile, hell collapses.

BIRTHDAY

Every day
is your birthday.

Today is a new day
and you are born again

with the sunrise
and with new opportunities.

Realize you are performing
a unique piece of music

that can never be written again,
entangled with your subjective web
of unrepeatable memories.

Every day is a gift
and a reminder

that you are a magnificent
and inexpressible miracle.

And this instant remembrance
was improbable from happening,

yet the universe
and you exist in it.

UNCONDITIONAL LOVE

You and I are messengers for duality.
All of us are
travelers on a cosmic journey.

All of us are stardust
salsa dancing in
whirlpools of nebulas,

flirting with
infinity and destiny.
Life is a dream
we wake up from.

And we're visitors
passing through
for a precious moment,
sharing our vulnerability
and realizing unconditional love can exist.

FREEDOM

Below the sun
and below the celestial ancestors
is humanity conceived
in the orgasm of birth.

We tear through into a massive
mystery of joy and suffering
to play a role in the influx
of creation and destruction.

Our cosmic inheritance
is to experience
the boundless beauty of life.
A marvelous sacrament
bellowed forth from the echoes
of chaos.

There are no adults here,
only wide-eyed, ill-tempered
and combustible children
playing and eroding in paradise.

We are the ever-growing
and ever-expanding child
that must learn to burn the metals
of vanity and fear
rooted inside.
To grow up and forge
the great sword of freedom—

Hold your sword high!
Freedom is digging into the nucleus of the self.
Knowing yourself is a constant process
that exceeds death.

III.
TRANSFORM

REMEMBER YOURSELF

Who I am today
is not the person I was yesterday.
Who I am today,
will never catch up
with the person I'll be tomorrow.

Who am I today
is created by remembering myself
in this passing moment,
remembering I am here
observing this mind, this body,
and this space I'm in,
and my experience within it.

Remember yourself as you are now.
Where are you now?
To remember yourself
is to focus your attention,
gather your energies,
and move toward
one center of awareness.

That center of awareness
is who I am.
And maybe who you are
is witnessing our ever-changing reactions
to an ever-changing phenomenon
that's out of our control.

GOD BLESS THE BREATH OF LIFE

God bless
our breath of life, as it is
a gift of fire
on the tongue
igniting the spirit to rise
and record our discord and create this
sublime instant.

God bless
our sacred union of self,
a gift of water
pouring down rain
on body and brain,
nurturing son and daughter,
mother and father,
and our holy gardens,
so peace may reign on earth!

God bless
all vibrations making love
to our spines and minds,
a gift of air
allowing all I am to come alive.
In the formless sounds
of newborn clouds
breathing and being—

God bless
all individual heartbeats
jumping to the sky
but preserving heaven below.
A gift of the earth,
speaking the way trees talk,

pumping blood as a collective organism.
No self to divide truth.
And if you want proof, it's in the nonverbals
of trees
giving oxygen to existence to be free!

God bless
our eyesight
to see we are always embedded in the sunlight
even when we're cloaked in darkness.

God bless
our consciousness,
the original observer
witnessing the purpose of life
in a single breath.

NAMING IT

I want to see beyond the skeletons,
beyond the marrow of this mystery,
with my own two eyes
the central self
that precedes reality.
To know there's a reason
for why *it is what it is.*
To know it's not meaningless,
not random cause and effect,
or forces of chaos
playing a game of chance.

I see what I see.
Heroes and villains
falling to their graves,
immersed in roles they don't believe in.
Winning and losing something
of value and meaning,
switching sides and drawing lines
just to cross them again.

I see what I see.
A universe making a farce
out of itself, words, nouns, persons,
places, and things.
And naming it *existence.*

I see what I see.
My sensitivity locked
in a skin suit,
a bundle of organs, blood, beliefs,
and emotions that I think are my own.
But I take notice of others

trapped in their sensitive skin suits—
a prison that we're hallucinating.

I see what I see.
I can never point you
in the right direction of my complete experience

of what it's like to be me
like the fact you'll never see your biological face
the way others see it.
Even if you look in the mirror twice.

I see what I see
like fragmented pictures and frames
taken from a camera.
If our perceptual filters
were purged and cleansed,
then the world of appearances
and the world of the unseen
would infuse and emerge
as it is: infinite.

One cannot speak, or conceptualize
the central self or their complete experiences of that core.
Therefore, one must surrender
to the silence of it.

TRANSFORMATION

One impossibility
in the natural world
is a dying cloud
diminished to nothing.

The cloud can only become
the receding rain and snow
transforming its form.
But it never dies.
It remains as its true nature—
one dynamic energy.

BREATHING IS LAW

Can living be as simple
       as breathing in fresh air?

I listen to the breeze
       and feel it touch my skin,
like the person I love most.

I watch the wind move the leaves.
       The leaves twist with the charm and precision
of a ballerina leaping into the sky!

The law of nature is
       breathe in and out,
take it all in, and let it go.

ARRIVING

Where is he at?

Is it fiction or fact?

Where did she go?

How do you know?

Is it me or you?

Is it one or two?

Humans are tantalizing riddles

within their own skins.

You and I are

one endless flux

of consciousness

changing in the present

arriving here and now.

SPIRIT SONGS

Birds sing
beautiful songs
of harmony.

A spirit song
evoking
melodies

of a unifying breath
of the universe.

Listen to the birds
sing at dawn.

And you may hear yourself
as *oneness*

discovered
in the pulse
of their soul language.

INVISIBLE SELF

Who am I?
But the one and many.

With your eyes closed,
feel the invisible current.

Pay attention and listen
to the vastness of the ocean
encompassed in a shallow shell.

There's no ocean to see
with your eyes,
but you know it is present inside.

Who am I?
But the one
ripple,
ocean
invisible
self.

DIVINE DEPARTURE

We the crowd of observers
watch with wonder,
catching a glimpse of
the cherry blossom parade.

We gander and glance at the slow fade,
a dance of the brittle birth and rise
and then the descent and decay—

the flow and fall of lathered leaves.
Kissing the space in between
heaven and earth.

We peeped the pink and white petals
on their way down
to carelessly caress the ground.

We are like the blushed leaves
caught in the ebb and breeze
of spring.
We are watching ourselves and
time melt
and slip away and sway, like
day breaking into a bruised night.

The crowd of visitors finish
participating
in the passage through the path
of life—
the departure and return
to our source of light.

WHEREVER YOU GO, THERE YOU ARE

Wherever you go, there you are
running in a perfect circle
enslaved in a perfect storm
attempting to escape this
wheel of suffering.

And you grasp harder
seeing how their faces
eventually wear out.
You grasp harder
seeing how their vitality
wears thin.

Wherever you go there you are
questioning the purpose of
this strange trip
that seems to go nowhere.
Old age confronts you in the mirror.
Sickness stares you down
with possibilities in its eyes.

Death removes your belongings
and expels your future
teaching you transcendence
and the truth about how to dance
like a mystic in bliss.

LOTUS BLOSSOM

I wrote this poem
as a dedication and admiration of gratitude.

To the shining ones
who came into being before time,
revealing the inner depths
of our infinite influx
and our essential self.

To the shinning ones
swimming in starlight streams
that seem to be at an endless distance.
Before the appearance of an aloof light
touched our eyes
and offered us a chance
to befriend the darkness.

This is an honorable tribute
to the shinning ones
revealing a path of love,
a way to be
the radiant lotus that blossoms
growing from the mud.

To the heights
beyond the heavens.
A true insight
into the nature of reality.
A chosen path
of dissolving the opposites
and spaces in between all things.
To be in divine union with all.
Thank you.

STREAM OF CONSCIOUSNESS

We are
      beautiful
           woman and man woven together as one
glorious life force.

In holy matrimony
           pervading
  matter and facts.
           Entranced in a mad hatter
daydream.

We make up
      every atom
 and fiber in the fabric
        of the universe.

You are the dawn
      of a new world
and you mean everything to me—

like the big bang,
      like the music you sang
that kept me sane.
      The yin to my yang.

SAKE POETRY PART 1

Dear Future Me,

You've pierced through reality's seams
inside the vision of your dreams.
Flying up high
like an orgasmic sigh
while on top of the world
giving her a whirl.

What was peeped and given
on the peaks of heaven?
Did you meet
celestial dragons,
the pantheon
of paragons,
the irresponsible elites?

Did you greet
human slaves
that kissed holy feet,
feet that seem
to never touch the ground?
Making the crowd
go *Wow*.
No defiance.
Only compliance.

Love yourself.

SAKE POETRY
PART 2

Dear Future Me,

What happened to your friends along the way?
Were they pretending to stay?
Did they want to break you down?
Abuse your feelings,
or did they want to take you down
from your ceilings,
as if you were a broken chandelier?
Did they appear to be sincere?

Or were they sinister snakes,
falsehoods and fakes,
catty catfishes
stealing birthday wishes?
Some bombastic facades,
plastic wannabe gods?
They weren't the same friends of your youth?
They couldn't handle your deepest truth?

Love yourself.

SAKE POETRY
PART 3

Dear Future Me,

Are you happy and strong?
What kept you going all along?
How is your mental health?
How is your soul's wealth?

Did you eat and take
everything on your plate
and transform your torture and pain,
your chaos and mistakes into a séance?

Spiritually and physically,
did you stay honest and convey
your soul effortlessly
to flow and pour out of you?

Did you cleanse your ego blues,
while making amends with the ego's ruse?
Did you finally accept our future death?
Did you clean up the messes in your mental rooms?

Did you break out of the illusions and institutions
of greed and wrath,
the ones that hold you and I back
in a straitjacket?
Provoking you to perform
a raging racket?

Did society change and rearrange
from a lonely and dark dystopia
into a collective dream utopia?

Love yourself.

P.S I offer up this Sake poetry
to you and me,

so we remain blessed
in the future where there's no stress.
   Remember our thesis:
as we thrive, we're still alive,
resting in peace not pieces.
We're all one under the sun.

INHERITED WILL

Fear of death is an old and natural impulse
we humans are consumed by.
This invisible and mysterious phenomenon
claimed our lives the second we opened our eyes
and cried and called for our mother's care.
Its presence was weighted on our mother's face
as she worried and watched our first steps.
Its presence stalks our vitality—
waiting, like a thief in a dark alleyway.

When do we die?
When a bullet, or blade pierces the heart?
When we're attacked by a global
and contagious virus?
When we stop breathing?
When the body is frozen and motionless?
When our consciousness fades
and the last glimmer of sentience
written on our faces is wiped away?

Does our soul live on
after it leaps out of our body?
This flesh wrapped around my inflamed exuberance
will perish,
but the dynamic passion that moves my heart
will never be extinguished!
The smoldering fire within will be passed on!
My dying wish for the human will to survive
and conquer their fears will be inherited.
I will never die, and my dreams will never end,
as long as you remember and keep me
in your memories.
Our souls live on!
We only die when we're forgotten.

THE GREAT BEYOND

An 80-year-old man
looks in the mirror and perceives
his body's personal prestige fading.
He touches his fragile face, and perceives his persona,
his self-deluded hallucination waning thin.

An 18-year-old man
looks in the mirror and sees his brisk smile
and endless youth glowing, like a full moon waxing.
He touches his bristle-covered face,
and like Narcissus he admires his own reflection,
and feels an infinite pleasure in the life he's living.

An 8-year-old boy
looks in the mirror while brushing his teeth, before bed
and wonders why he's alive, and what if he was never born?
These questions are like shadows making movements in a fermented fog;
the answers are near but appear to be invisible.

What would happen if
the elderly man, the young man,
and little boy all die?
What would they lose?
All they lose is the present moment.
All that disappears is this present moment.

YOGA

We're born from the same eternal womb
and die in the same mortal tomb.

But before the finale we go clockwise
on a rotating wheel of time

moving through our central spine
searching for the infinite prize.

Along the way
our organs get entangled in circles
caught in countless hurdles.

We experience heaven and hell
as a dream under the blue moon.
Our bodies fade, fuse and attune
to experience the sorcerer's spell.

In our essence
we stretch and breathe, and bleed
with hearts on sleeves.

All of existence,
plus you and me.
We are the same.
Been playing a game
of hide and seek, to see
the divine union with ourselves.

ALREADY DEAD LIVE NOW

The mighty animal king has arisen
to the occasion of
gnawing its prey,
chewing and crunching it into pieces.
With blood-stained teeth,
flesh crumbles like mountains,
bones are ground into powder.
It sounds like the inescapable
wrath of the brutal truth that
life is impermanent.

This terror of death sits
at our bedside during the hour of dusk.
Some of us are lucky enough
to hypnotize and distract ourselves
from the vivid sounds
of our mutable nature.

Are they really lucky?
Do they celebrate life,
or do they cling to the fear
of losing everything they possess?
Losing it to what comes after,
the plunge into the unknown.

The terror of death is exposed
in the demise of your
self-created allegorical mind
that is gone in a snap
of your fingers.

Death sings her verses of surrender
so we remember it's only change and transition.
Our mortal bodies have already been
embraced by the hands of fate.
She held us as a newborn,
grasping us as delicate fruits of knowledge,

knowing the fruitful will one day
decay and perish with time.

Don't try to time travel to the future,
or step backwards into the past
with your mind.
What are your hands touching?
Where are your feet gently planted?
Take it all in minute by minute,
day by day.
Tomorrow isn't promised.
Live now and appreciate
what doesn't last.

THE END

Life is death's twin and can't be true
without the existence of the other.
She was an angel of death
that kissed my forehead.
She kissed me for good fortune
for the long-endeavoring life
I was about to embark on.

I became aware of her
as she gently grasped my hand.
We were standing in a mesmerizing meadow.
Her hair looked like flames.
She held a scythe and a smile across her face.

I never thought death would be so beautiful.
Death held up an all-seeing mirror to my eyes
that reflected past versions of myself, and past deeds.
And in this luminosity of deep contemplation
I weighed the consequences of what I've done
and the choices I've made.

Death said to me,
You've spent your whole life
running away from yourself
and your mortality.
And it's finally caught up with you
to tell you, I love you.

You were always enough.
You were the one.
An individual wave of water
compared to the vast sea
of various perceptions.

Now you return to the eternal sea.
No point of view to consume you.
All we could hear was silence.
All we could feel was peace.

ABOUT THE AUTHOR

Austin Lamar Dumas is a poet and artist living in Edmond, OK. He's the author of a short collection of poetry called *Hocus Pocus Here We Go*, which is on Amazon. He spends his time pondering the big questions in life while enjoying this wild adventure before it's dust dancing in the wind.
Find him and his mystical musings on Instagram @dumasism and Facebook FB: AustinDumas.

www.ingramcontent.com/pod-product-compliance
Lightning Source LLC
LaVergne TN
LVHW051747080426
835511LV00018B/3254